SUBJECT

THIS NOTEBOOK BELONGS TO

DATE STARTED

DATE FINISHED

CUES

Write yourself CUES to help you understand and highlight important information, and to review & study in the future. For example:

What's the main idea or focus of the notes?

What exam question(s) do the notes suggest to you?

Write prompts to jog your memory at study time.

THE CORNELL NOTE-TAKING METHOD EXPLAINED

CLASS, TOPIC, DATE

NOTES - TAKEN DURING CLASS

Record the lecture in a way that makes sense to you. For Example:

use Bullets

Write Down the Main Points

Draw Charts & Diagrams & Formulas

use Abbreviations & Paraphrase

use Topic Headers

Leave Blank Lines Between Subjects

Put a ☆ Beside Really Important Stuff

SUMMARY

Write up a page summary after class. Include the main points / major ideas so you can quickly and efficiently find important information later.

PERSONAL INDEX

1

2

3

4

5

6

7

8

9

10

11

12

13

14

15

16

17

18

19

20

21

22

23

24

25

26

27

28

29

30

PERSONAL INDEX

31	46
32	47
33	48
34	49
35	50
36	51
37	52
38	53
39	54
40	55
41	56
42	57
43	58
44	59
45	60

PERSONAL INDEX

61

62

63

64

65

66

67

68

69

70

71

72

73

74

75

76

77

78

79

80

81

82

83

84

85

86

87

88

89

90

PERSONAL INDEX

91

82

93

94

95

96

97

98

99

100

101

102

103

104

105

106

107

108

109

110

111

112

113

114

115

116

117

118

119

120

Made in the USA
Las Vegas, NV
22 September 2021